VOLCANOES

Anna Claybourne

KINGFISHER

KINGFISHER

Kingfisher Publications Plc
New Penderel House
283–288 High Holborn
London WC1V 7HZ
www.kingfisherpub.com

First published by Kingfisher Publications Plc 2007
10 9 8 7 6 5 4 3 2 1
1TR/0507/GCUP/UNITED(UNITED)/140MA/F

For Q2A Media
Editor: Honor Head
Consultant: Terry Jennings
Designer: Chhaya Sajwan
Art director: Rahul Dhiman
Illustrators: Rishi Bhardwaj, Amit Tayal, Aadil A Siddiqui
  and Subhash C Vohra
Image researcher: Jyoti Sachdev

For Kingfisher
Editorial manager: Russell McLean
Art director: Mike Davis
DTP manager: Nicky Studdart
Senior production controller: Lindsey Scott

Printed in China

NOTE TO READERS
The website addresses listed in this book are correct at the time
of going to print. However, due to the ever-changing nature of the
internet, website addresses and content can change. Websites can
contain links that are unsuitable for children. The publisher cannot
be held responsible for changes in website addresses or content, or
for information obtained through third-party websites. We strongly
advise that internet searches should be supervised by an adult.

CONTENTS

Kilauea
The most active volcano in the world is Kilauea on the island of Hawaii.

NORTH AMERICA

Mount St Helens
Washington State, USA

PACIFIC OCEAN

Surtsey
Iceland

Surtsey
In 1963 the volcanic island of Surtsey appeared out of the sea near Iceland.

Paricutín
Mexico

ATLANTIC OCEAN

Kilauea
Hawaii

WORLD OF VOLCANOES

Arenal
Costa Rica

Mount Pelée
Martinique, West Indies

Nevado del Ruiz
Colombia

SOUTH AMERICA

At any given time, at least 20 active volcanoes are erupting around the world. Right now hot, molten rock from deep inside the Earth is bursting out of the ground. It breaks up into choking black volcanic ash that fills the air, or flows down the mountain slopes, burning trees, crops and even animals and people.

Deadly disasters
As well as showering its surroundings with seething lava at a temperature of over 1,000°C – ten times hotter than a boiling kettle – an exploding volcano flings out rocks, ash, mud and poisonous gases. Volcanoes have caused many of the most famous and deadly natural disasters in the history of the Earth.

Rich growth
Volcanoes are not all bad news. Volcanic eruptions build new mountains and create land out of the sea. Many rocks and minerals formed inside volcanoes are useful and valuable to us. Throughout the ages, people who live near volcanoes have found that the soil is excellent for growing crops, due to the mineral-rich ash that falls onto it.

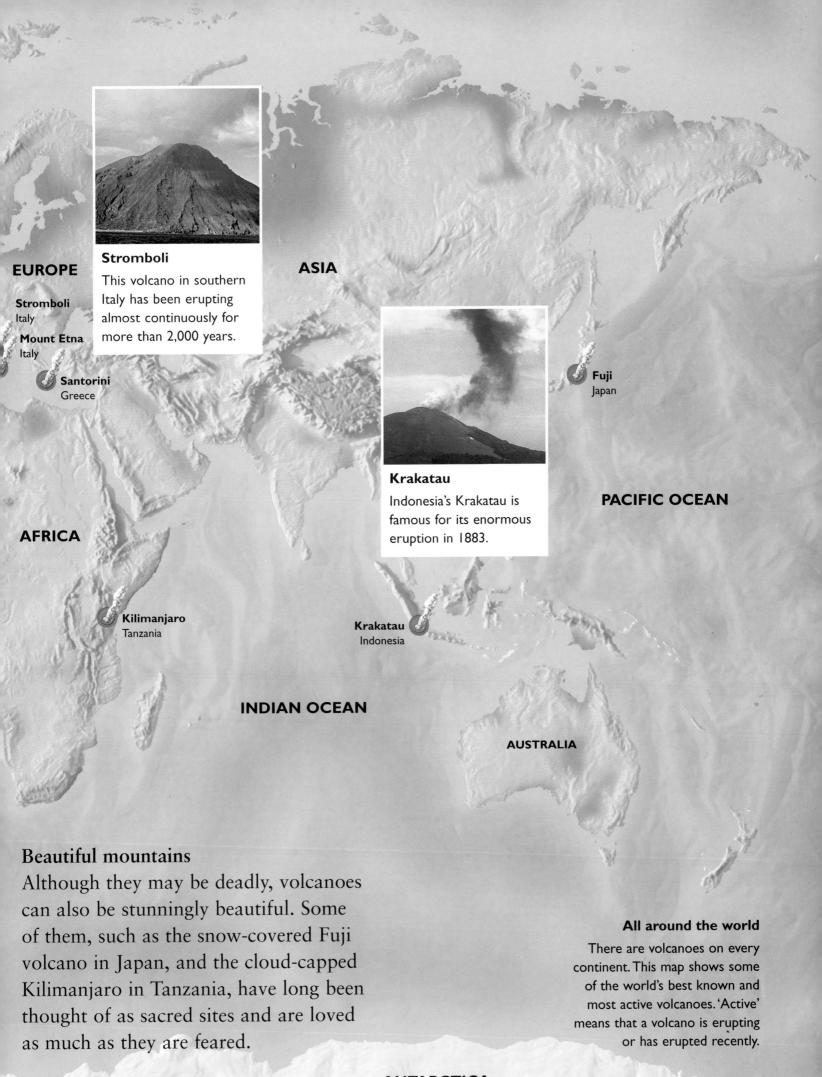

EUROPE

ASIA

Stromboli
Italy

Mount Etna
Italy

Santorini
Greece

Stromboli
This volcano in southern Italy has been erupting almost continuously for more than 2,000 years.

Krakatau
Indonesia's Krakatau is famous for its enormous eruption in 1883.

Fuji
Japan

PACIFIC OCEAN

AFRICA

Kilimanjaro
Tanzania

Krakatau
Indonesia

INDIAN OCEAN

AUSTRALIA

Beautiful mountains
Although they may be deadly, volcanoes can also be stunningly beautiful. Some of them, such as the snow-covered Fuji volcano in Japan, and the cloud-capped Kilimanjaro in Tanzania, have long been thought of as sacred sites and are loved as much as they are feared.

All around the world
There are volcanoes on every continent. This map shows some of the world's best known and most active volcanoes. 'Active' means that a volcano is erupting or has erupted recently.

ANTARCTICA

Eruption!

Some volcanoes erupt slowly. Their lava seeps to the surface in a constant, gentle flow. But the classic volcanic eruption is a sudden, violent explosion. Before such an eruption happens, magma – molten rock from inside the Earth – pushes upwards and collects under the volcano. Once it leaves the volcano, magma is called lava.

Under pressure

As the pressure of the magma builds up underneath, lava may begin to leak out of the sides of the volcano, which can start to bulge and shake. These signs warn that it is about to erupt. When the volcano finally blows its top, hot lava, ash, rocks, gas and dust burst out with an enormous roar.

Ash cloud

As lava comes to the surface, it can cool, harden and shatter, forming volcanic ash. A powerful eruption can throw burning hot ash, mixed with dust, gas and mud, several kilometres into the air.

River of fire

Boiling hot liquid lava flows down the sides of the volcano, forming lava rivers and pools. Because it is thick and sticky, it usually flows quite slowly.

Hurling rocks

When a volcano erupts, a huge amount of energy is released. As the pressurized magma and gas suddenly escape and expand, ash, dust and chunks of solid rock are hurled high into the sky. An eruption releases vast amounts of heat, too.

Incredible energy

The eruption of Krakatau in 1883 is thought to have released 200 megatons of energy – the equivalent of 15,000 nuclear bombs. Volcanic energy also takes the form of sound. The explosion of Krakatau made a boom that could be heard on the island of Rodriguez, around 4,800km away. Volcanoes are too dangerous and unpredictable for us to be able to harness much of their energy.

Rocks, bombs and blocks

As a volcano erupts, it blows up solid rock from the outside of the mountain, forcing pebbles and boulders into the air. Lava can also cool and harden as it flies through the air, forming solid lumps known as volcanic bombs or blocks.

The aftermath

A big volcanic eruption can go on for hours, days or weeks. Afterwards, the countryside, towns and villages nearby may be unrecognizable. Sometimes, a layer of ash and dust settles onto the landscape, choking plants and animals, blocking roads and ruining homes.

Path of destruction

Flows of lava and hot ash burn everything in their path to cinders, reducing forests, prairies and fields of crops to blackened wasteland. It can take many years for an area devastated by a volcanic eruption to recover fully.

Mudflow mayhem
Mud can be a deadly result of an eruption. Sometimes, mudflows engulf towns and drown thousands of people.

Death and disaster

Although volcanic eruptions are loud, fiery and violent, the actual eruption itself rarely kills many people. This is because the centre of the eruption is usually at the top of a mountain, away from settlements, and there is usually some warning.

Choking and suffocating

Yet the results of a volcano can cause mass destruction. Fine ash falling onto a town or village can choke and suffocate people and animals. Volcanic landslides and mudflows may flatten villages and farms. Big volcanic eruptions can also send shock waves into the sea, creating lethal tsunamis. And if a volcano wipes out crops and livestock, the local people may suffer a deadly famine.

Coated in ash
In 1991, the eruption of Mount Pinatubo in the Philippines left a layer of ash 2m deep over a radius of 3km around the volcano. Further away, streets and cars were covered in enough ash to make travel impossible.

Flattened by the blast
Hot lava and ash, flying rocks and landslides can leave a forest burned, blackened and barren following a volcanic eruption.

EXPLODING EARTH

In March 1980, Mount St Helens, a beautiful snow-capped volcano in the USA, suddenly started to tremble. Slowly, its north side began to bulge outwards as it prepared to erupt. Finally, at 8.32am on 18 May, the volcano blew up with a massive boom. It was a spectacular eruption, but why did it happen?

Underground studies

Volcanoes are difficult to study. They are dangerous and the events that make the explosions happen take place deep underground. But scientists have discovered a lot about how volcanoes work, and why they come in so many different sizes, shapes and styles.

Rivers of rock

Pyroclastic flows can surge forwards at speeds of up to 240km/h. It is impossible to outrun them or drive away from them. Searing heat, poisonous gas and choking dust make them deadly for any living thing caught in their path.

Blowing apart

When the crust of rock covering the north side of Mount St Helens fell away, a high-pressure mixture of hot magma (molten rock), ash and superheated steam inside was released and burst outwards. Some of the material rose into the air in vast clouds, while the rest formed rivers of hot ash, small rocks and gases known as pyroclastic flows.

Death and destruction

The deadly rivers thundered down the volcano's steep slopes, obliterating everything in their path. The area had been evacuated, but 57 people were killed, including a volcanologist (volcano scientist), David Johnston, who had gone to observe the volcano. The eruption also killed thousands of deer and elk and destroyed roads, railways, homes and farmland.

Changing shape

The 1980 eruption of Mount St Helens lasted for over nine hours and blew away a huge chunk of the mountain. These pictures show its shape before the explosion (top) and afterwards (above).

Inside a volcano

Most volcanoes are mountains. This is because as a volcano erupts, lava, ash and rock pile up and cool all around it, building it higher and higher. Unlike a normal mountain, which is just a mound of rock, a volcano has a channel, called a vent, that leads right into the Earth. When a volcano is 'dormant' (sleeping) or when an active volcano is not erupting, the top of the vent may be blocked with cooled, hardened lava. But underneath, hot magma is collecting, ready for the next eruption.

Bombs

Blocks

Bombs and blocks

Bombs and blocks are big pieces of rock and lava that are thrown out of a volcano. Blocks are solid chunks of rock and can be as big as a bus. Bombs are smaller and made of semi-molten lava. They often form a teardrop shape as they fly through the air.

Active craters

The crater of a volcano, such as this one in Vanuatu in the Pacific Ocean, usually looks like a huge, gaping, bowl-shaped hollow. Steam and gas may pour from the crater, even when the volcano is not erupting.

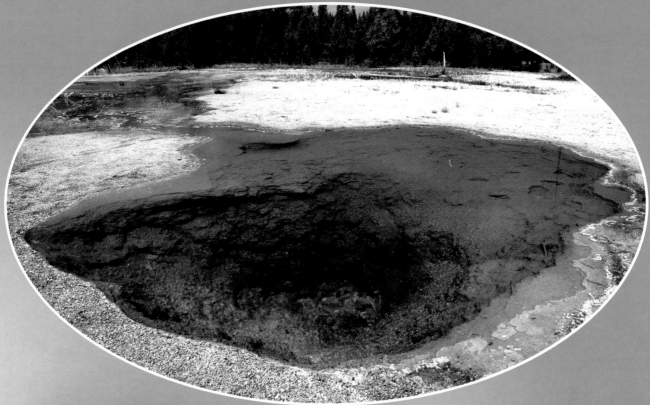

Volcanic water features

The hot underground magma in volcanic areas often heats up water under the ground. The heated water rises to the surface in the form of a hot spring (above), a jet of steam called a fumarole, or a hot fountain called a geyser.

The parts of a volcano

In the ground underneath a volcano is a magma chamber – a huge mass of hot, melted rock. The magma pushes towards the surface up a tube called a pipe. This leads into the vent, which travels up the middle of the volcano. The top of the vent opens out into the crater, where lava flows out of the volcano. It may also flow out through smaller side vents, called dykes. The volcano's flanks (slopes) are made up of layers of old, cooled lava from previous eruptions.

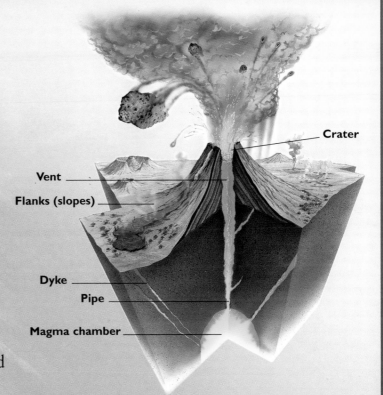

Crater

Vent

Flanks (slopes)

Dyke

Pipe

Magma chamber

Red-hot lava

When molten rock is inside the Earth, it is called magma. Once it emerges through the Earth's surface during a volcanic eruption, it is known as lava. Most of the rock just under the Earth's surface is not molten magma, but harder, more solid rock. The magma is found only in certain parts of the Earth. It moves up through a weakness in the Earth's crust and forces its way to the surface, forming volcanoes.

Types of lava

There are several different types of lava, depending on the type of rocks it is made of. For example, felsic lavas contain the minerals quartz and feldspar, and are thick and sticky, while mafic lavas contain basalt rock and are thin and runny. Scientists have found that the type of lava in a volcano plays a large part in the way it erupts.

Slow or sudden?

If the lava is very thick and sticky, it cannot flow fast. Gases get trapped in it and it builds up in a high-pressure mass, before exploding. In a 'Plinian-type' eruption, the volcano explodes, turning the thick lava to ash. In a 'Strombolian-type' eruption, big lumps of thick, sticky lava fly out of the volcano. Thin, runny lava leads to gentler 'Hawaiian-type' eruptions. The lava forms fountains, puddles and streams as it flows smoothly from the volcano.

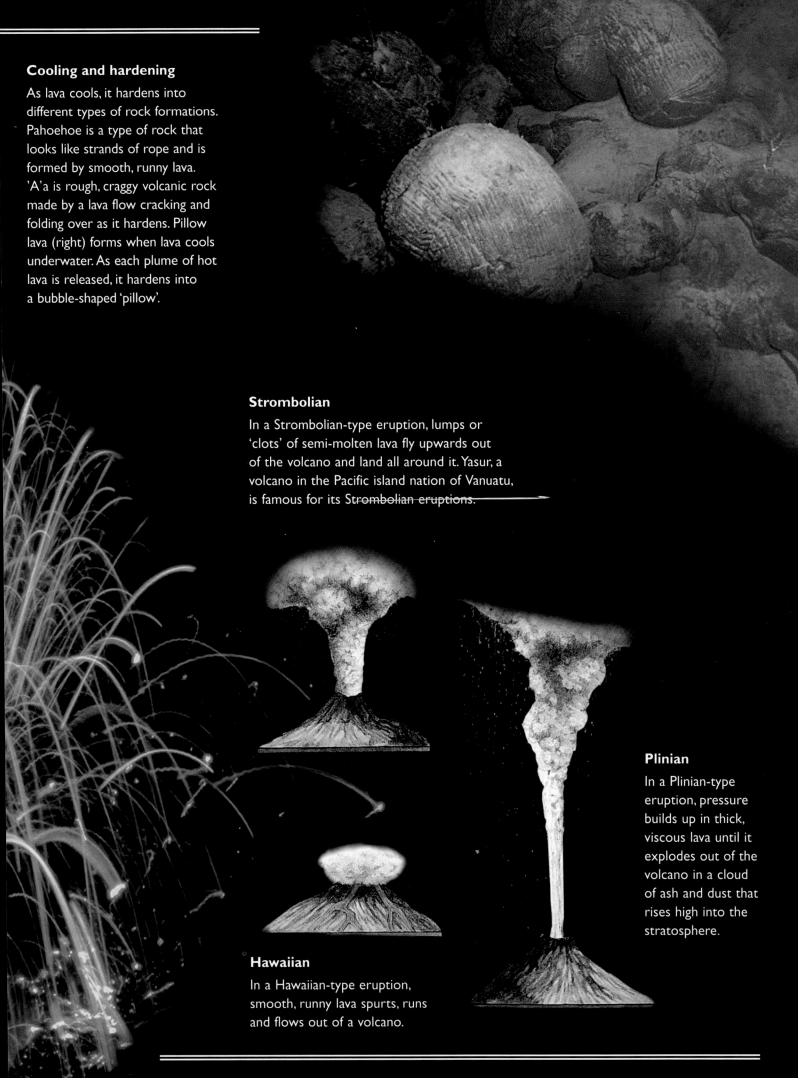

Cooling and hardening

As lava cools, it hardens into different types of rock formations. Pahoehoe is a type of rock that looks like strands of rope and is formed by smooth, runny lava. 'A'a is rough, craggy volcanic rock made by a lava flow cracking and folding over as it hardens. Pillow lava (right) forms when lava cools underwater. As each plume of hot lava is released, it hardens into a bubble-shaped 'pillow'.

Strombolian

In a Strombolian-type eruption, lumps or 'clots' of semi-molten lava fly upwards out of the volcano and land all around it. Yasur, a volcano in the Pacific island nation of Vanuatu, is famous for its Strombolian eruptions.

Plinian

In a Plinian-type eruption, pressure builds up in thick, viscous lava until it explodes out of the volcano in a cloud of ash and dust that rises high into the stratosphere.

Hawaiian

In a Hawaiian-type eruption, smooth, runny lava spurts, runs and flows out of a volcano.

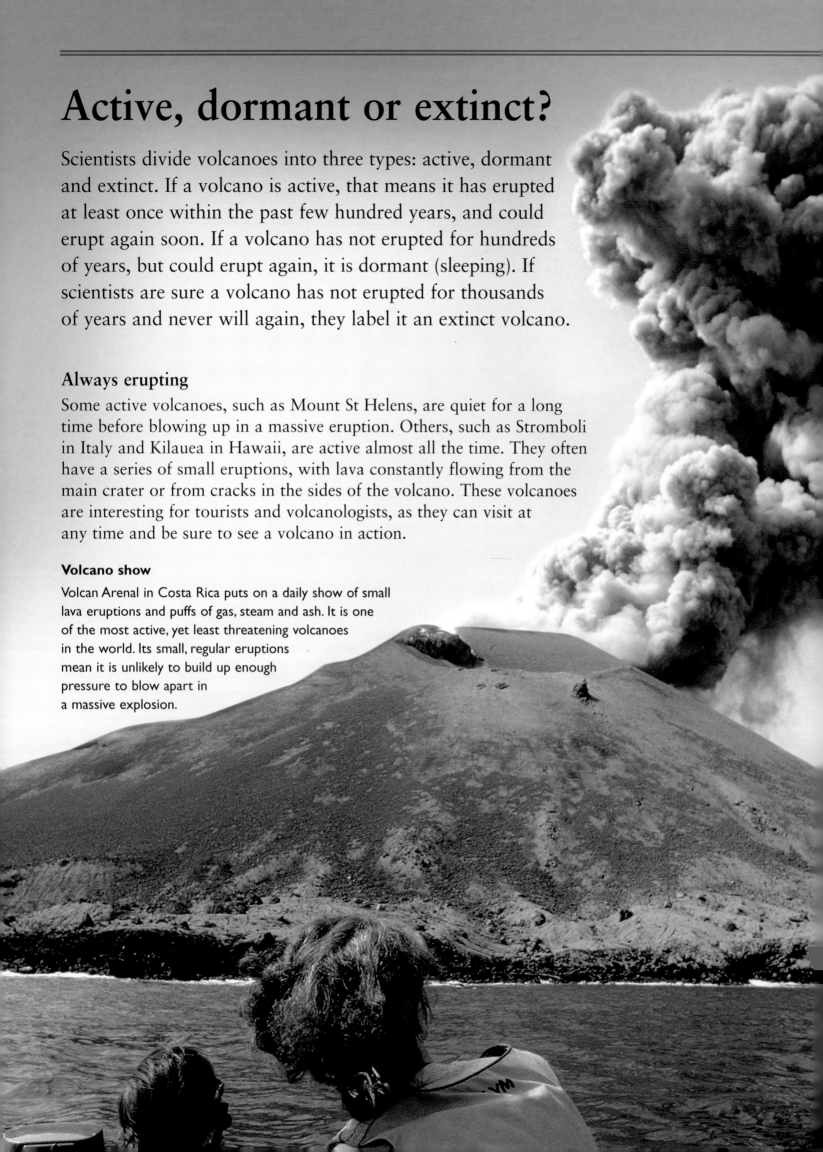

Active, dormant or extinct?

Scientists divide volcanoes into three types: active, dormant and extinct. If a volcano is active, that means it has erupted at least once within the past few hundred years, and could erupt again soon. If a volcano has not erupted for hundreds of years, but could erupt again, it is dormant (sleeping). If scientists are sure a volcano has not erupted for thousands of years and never will again, they label it an extinct volcano.

Always erupting

Some active volcanoes, such as Mount St Helens, are quiet for a long time before blowing up in a massive eruption. Others, such as Stromboli in Italy and Kilauea in Hawaii, are active almost all the time. They often have a series of small eruptions, with lava constantly flowing from the main crater or from cracks in the sides of the volcano. These volcanoes are interesting for tourists and volcanologists, as they can visit at any time and be sure to see a volcano in action.

Volcano show

Volcan Arenal in Costa Rica puts on a daily show of small lava eruptions and puffs of gas, steam and ash. It is one of the most active, yet least threatening volcanoes in the world. Its small, regular eruptions mean it is unlikely to build up enough pressure to blow apart in a massive explosion.

Kilauea's crater

Although Kilauea in Hawaii is probably the world's most active volcano, you can walk right up to the edge of its crater. Its most recent eruption, called the Pu'u 'O'o eruption, has been going on continuously since 1983.

Deceptively dormant

It can be very hard to tell the difference between a dormant volcano and an extinct volcano. Most people thought Vesuvius, a famous volcano in Italy, was extinct before it blew up in 79CE, killing around 3,500 people.

Volcano shapes

On Hawaii's Big Island stands the world's largest active volcano, Mauna Loa. But Mauna Loa is not a great big pointed cone, it is a massive, flattened hump, stretching over a vast area 120km long and 103km wide. Mauna Loa is a shield volcano – so-called because it resembles a huge, curved shield lying on the ground. The shape of a volcano is decided by the way it erupts and the type of lava that flows from it. The three main volcano shapes are shield, cinder cone and stratovolcano.

Shaped by lava

Volcanoes are built by the lava, ash and rock that come out of them. If the lava is thin and runny, it flows gently out of the volcano as in Hawaiian-type eruptions, and runs a long way before it cools and hardens. It spreads out over a wide area, creating a broad, gently sloping shield volcano. Strombolian-type eruptions throw out lots of small lumps of lava, which build up to form a steep-sided cone shape with a wide crater – a cinder cone volcano. Stratovolcanoes can erupt suddenly, after a long silence, with a Plinian-type eruption of thick, sticky lava. Lava, ash and rock build up around the crater, making a sharply pointed volcano with slightly curving sides.

Shield volcano
Runny lava spreads out as it flows gently from the volcano to form a low, flat mound.

Tall and pointed
Mount Fuji in Japan is a stratovolcano made up of layers of cooled lava, ash and debris deposited by ash falls and pyroclastic flows.

Cinder cone volcano

Repeated small, violent eruptions blast a wide crater and build up layers of lava and cinders into a cone shape. Of the three main shapes, cinder cones are the smallest and most common.

Stratovolcano

Large, explosive eruptions of sticky lava build up a pointed spout around the crater. The mountain is formed from layers of ash, rock and lava.

Shallow slopes

The wide, dark hill of Mauna Loa looms over Big Island in Hawaii. As well as being the world's largest active volcano, Mauna Loa is also the world's biggest (though not highest) mountain. It has erupted more than 30 times since its recorded activity began in 1843.

How a caldera is made

Sometimes, a volcano erupts so violently that a huge chunk of the mountain is blown away (1), leaving a ring-shaped hollow called a caldera (2). The caldera often fills with water, making a crater lake (3).

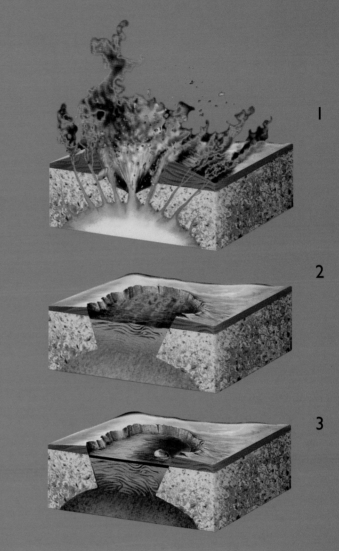

1

2

3

The Greek island of Santorini is an island caldera left by the eruption of a huge volcano in about 1630BCE.

FAMOUS ERUPTIONS

On 27 August 1883, the island volcano of
Krakatau, in Indonesia, blew itself to pieces.
The huge explosion was one of the biggest
volcanic eruptions in history. Even though
the island was uninhabited, the eruption
claimed the lives of at least 36,000 people
as a result of the showers of burning ash
and the huge tsunamis it caused.

Before and after

The 1883 eruption changed the shape of
Krakatau island completely. The top picture
shows it before the eruption and the
bottom picture after the eruption.

Krakatau explodes

The 1883 eruption of Krakatau was not caught on camera
because photography was still in its early stages. However,
many people witnessed it and the explosion was recorded
in the form of paintings, engravings and woodcuts.

Killer Krakatau

How did Krakatau kill so many people? First, the explosion hurled burning rock and volcanic ash into the air, which wiped out thousands of people – for example, all 3,000 inhabitants on the nearby island of Sebesi were killed. Second, as the volcano blew apart, its north side collapsed into the sea, creating a giant tsunami. The tsunami waves spread out across the Indian Ocean, reaching 40m high near some coasts. They devastated coastal towns and villages, and upturned boats, which killed thousands more people.

Laki: Destroying a nation

How can a volcano cause starvation? This is what happened at Laki in southern Iceland in 1783, when a volcanic fissure, or crack in the ground, opened up and began to erupt. The Laki eruption went on for over eight months and produced 14km^3 (cubic kilometres) of lava – the most lava ever recorded from a single eruption. It also released poisonous gases and clouds of choking ash and dust. Though there was no single, big explosion, this disastrous eruption killed a quarter of Iceland's population.

The Laki fissure

The Laki eruption did not burst out of the top of a single volcano. Instead it came from a long fissure that opened up in the ground, with at least 130 separate craters along it churning out lava and hot gases. Today, the fissure can still be seen as a series of cinder cones.

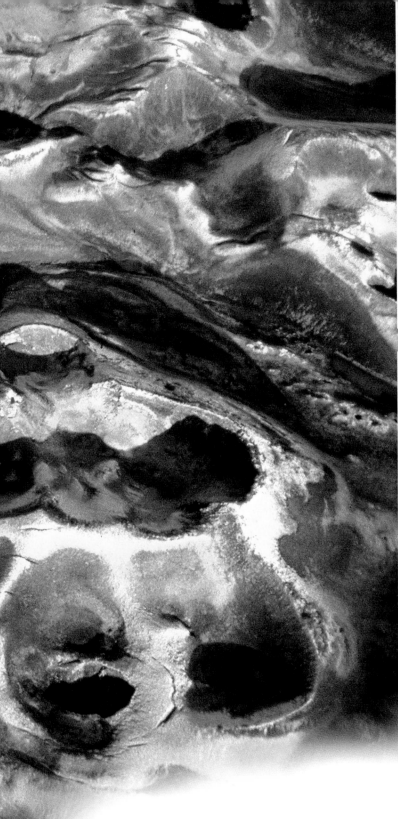

Freezing winters

The Laki eruption released so much gas into the atmosphere that it affected the climate, making the winter of 1783–84 unusually cold across North America and northern Europe.

Divided island

This map shows how Iceland is split by the Mid-Atlantic Ridge, shown in yellow. The Mid-Atlantic Ridge is a boundary between two of the huge tectonic plates (see page 33) that make up the Earth's crust. Where the plates meet, there is a lot of volcanic activity.

Suffocating and starving

Hundreds of people died in the Laki eruption as a result of lava flows, choking dust, poison gases and floods caused by melting ice. But worse was to come. One of the volcanic gases spewed out by the eruption was fluorine. It seeped across the countryside and was absorbed into grass and other plants. When farm animals ate the grass, they were poisoned and died. Over three-quarters of Iceland's cattle and sheep – 200,000 animals – were killed, leading to a famine that wiped out 9,000 people. Records show that death rates peaked in other northern countries too, so pollution from the eruption probably claimed thousands more lives elsewhere.

Ruiz: Rivers of mud

Nevado del Ruiz, a volcano in Colombia, has unleashed deadly lahars, or mudflows, onto the surrounding villages three times. In the first eruption, in 1595, 600 people died. In the second, in 1845, over 1,000 were killed. Then, on 13 November 1985, the volcano erupted again. When a rain of ash and dust fell on the town of Armero, 74km from the summit, the people wondered if they should evacuate – but the ash fall stopped and so they stayed. Then at 11pm that night, a rushing, roaring wall of mud, laden with rocks and boulders, descended on the town, smashing its buildings and drowning 23,000 of its inhabitants.

Armero: the aftermath

The day after the 1985 eruption of Nevado del Ruiz, this was all that remained of the town of Armero. It had been built on top of the old, hardened mudflow from Ruiz's previous major eruption in 1845. The 1985 mudflow took exactly the same path, drowning most of the town.

Rainstorm eruptions

Volcanic lahars happen when boiling lava, or a pyroclastic flow of hot rocks and ash, combines with water to create a hot, fast-moving river of mud. Lahars can result from a volcanic eruption during a heavy rainstorm. More often, as in the case of Nevado del Ruiz, the hot lava and ash melt the volcano's cap of snow and ice to create a torrent of water.

Fast-flowing danger

The mud in a lahar is runny, not thick and sticky. It surges down the mountain's river valleys at speeds of up to 100km/h – and the lahar may be so big that it can engulf a medium-sized town, such as Armero, in a few minutes. Even so, Armero's residents could have escaped by walking less than 1km to higher ground if they had known the mud was coming. Modern satellite warning systems would probably be able to prevent a disaster like this one happening again by giving the local people enough warning to flee.

Nevado del Ruiz

Nevado del Ruiz, a stratovolcano, is Colombia's highest active volcano, at 5,389m. The disastrous eruption of 1985 was its most recent, but it could erupt again.

Helping survivors

A rescuer helps a survivor of the 1985 Nevado del Ruiz disaster.

Pompeii: Entombed in ash

If you visit the remains of Pompeii, near Naples in Italy, you will see a Roman city preserved in every detail. Streets, houses, shops, theatres, wall paintings and everyday objects were frozen in time when the nearby volcano Vesuvius erupted in 79CE. After the first eruption threw a column of ash into the sky, pyroclastic flows engulfed the city in a layer of hot ash and dust up to 7m deep. Anyone who had not left when the volcano began to rumble and the first rocks and ash fell, was killed instantly by the deadly, choking dust.

Violent Vesuvius

The eruption of Vesuvius was violent and powerful – it was a Plinian-type eruption. These eruptions get their name from the philosopher Pliny's description of Vesuvius.

Body casts

When pyroclastic flows burst into Pompeii, everything was covered with ash, which later cooled and solidified. The bodies of the victims caught in the ash eventually rotted away, leaving empty hollows. Plaster casts made from these hollows reveal the shapes of the people and animals in their dying moments.

According to Pliny

The remains of Pompeii tell their own story, but we also have a written account of the eruption by the Roman philosopher Pliny the Younger. When Vesuvius began to erupt on 24 August, Pliny was staying with his uncle, Pliny the Elder, at Misenum, across the bay from Pompeii.

Crying out

When they saw the volcano begin to erupt, Pliny the Elder set off by boat to observe the eruption and rescue friends. He landed at Stabiae, near Pompeii, and found his friend Pomponianus, but they could not escape. Pliny the Elder died, along with over 2,000 of Pompeii's residents. Pliny the Younger escaped. He wrote: "You could hear the shrieks of women, the wailing of infants, and the shouting of men; some were calling their parents, others their children or their wives."

Uncovering Pompeii

For centuries, Pompeii lay buried beneath its layer of ash, and vineyards were planted on top. In 1594, workers digging a new canal discovered some of the ruins, but it was not until the 18th century that archaeologists began to excavate and uncover the whole city. Today, Pompeii is a huge tourist attraction.

Mount Pelée: Deadly gas

In late April 1902, Mount Pelée, on the French Caribbean island of Martinique, began to erupt. St Pierre, the prosperous town on the coast below the volcano, was showered with ash and enveloped in a smelly cloud of sulphur. Then, poisonous snakes and insects invaded the city, driven away from the mountainside by the earthquakes and ash falls. Dozens of people died from snake bites.

Deadly mistake

When a lahar, or mudflow, killed 23 workers in a factory north of the city on 5 May, people began to talk of escaping to another town on the island, Forte-de-France. But the governor declared the volcano, and St Pierre, to be safe. In fact, many people from surrounding villages crowded into the city, convinced it was the safest place to be. They were very, very wrong.

Powerful Pelée

The blast of hot gas, rocks and ash was so forceful that it knocked down all the walls in its path. It even toppled a 3-tonne statue and carried it 16m away. Most of the people, if they were not crushed by falling buildings, were killed by the intense heat of the burning gas.

The gas strikes

The townspeople of St Pierre tried to get on with their lives, but on 8 May at 7.50am Mount Pelée erupted again, this time with more force than ever. A terrifying pyroclastic flow of red-hot, glowing gases, ash and stones rolled down the mountain at 100km/h, directly onto St Pierre. Almost the entire population of 20,000, plus an extra 8,000 people who had come to the city for safety, were suffocated and burned alive by the deadly gas.

A few survivors

Sailors on ships moored in the harbour stared in horror as the city was destroyed, just before the ball of gas spread out across the water and enveloped the boats as well. On land only two people survived. One was a prisoner, Louis-Auguste Cyparis. He was being held in the city dungeon and survived because the tiny grate connecting his cell to the outside world let in only a little of the hot gas – enough to burn him, but not to kill him.

A narrow escape
Louis-Auguste Cyparis survived the eruption. He was pardoned and became a circus showman.

Gas cloud in Cameroon
In 1986, Cameroon's Lake Nyos, a lake in the middle of a volcanic crater, released a cloud of about $1km^3$ of suffocating carbon dioxide gas. As carbon dioxide is heavier than air, it rolled downhill and over the village of Lower Nyos, killing hundreds of people and animals.

29

CHANGING LANDSCAPES

One day in 1943, as Mexican farmer Dionisio Pulido worked in his cornfield, he saw the flat ground heave, swell and crack open before his eyes. Smoke, ash and then lava began to erupt from the hole as Pulido ran for his life. What he had seen was the birth of a brand-new volcano, Paricutín.

Something from nothing

Volcanoes are creators as well as destroyers. They can build new land and reshape the Earth's surface, form new rocks and renew the soil. And they work fast – all this can happen in minutes, hours or days, instead of the thousands of years it takes for mountains and rocks to be shaped by glaciers, wind and water erosion.

Swamped steeple

Lava and ash from the birth of Paricutín covered the nearby village of San Juan. All that could still be seen was the church, sticking up through a sea of cooled, broken lava.

New landscape

The eruption of Paricutín meant that people could no longer live in the nearby villages as their homes were destroyed. Where the villages once stood there is now a mass of craggy, cooled lava.

Birth and death

Paricutín erupted from 1943 to 1952. Over the first 24 hours, the eruption created a 50m cinder cone, as high as a 16-storey tower block. Paricutín was especially exciting for volcanologists. For the first time it allowed them to watch a volcano being born, growing and eventually becoming extinct – they were able to witness the entire life cycle of a volcano.

Tourists gaze at the spectacle of Paricutín erupting.

This chart shows how Paricutín grew over its nine-year eruption, from 1943 to 1952. It grew fast to begin with, then gradually slowed down.

Growth of a volcano

I day	50m high
I week	100m
I year	336m
9 years (final height)	424m

Shaping the Earth

Millions of years of volcanic eruptions have shaped much of the Earth's landscape. Even in places where there are no active volcanoes, you can see mountains and hills that are the remains of old volcanoes. When a volcano erupts, it can change the horizon overnight, by adding to its own height or blowing itself apart. And in the oceans, constant volcanic eruptions create new seabed.

Jigsaw Earth

The Earth is covered with a rocky, solid crust floating on top of hot, molten and semi-molten magma. This crust is divided into several huge pieces, like the pieces of a jigsaw, called tectonic plates. The plates are constantly moving, because of volcanic activity around their edges, or 'plate boundaries'. There are two main types of plate boundary. At spreading ridges, magma pushes out from inside the Earth and forms new crust. As it spreads out, it pushes the plates apart. At subduction zones, one plate plunges under another deep into the Earth, where it melts and forms new magma.

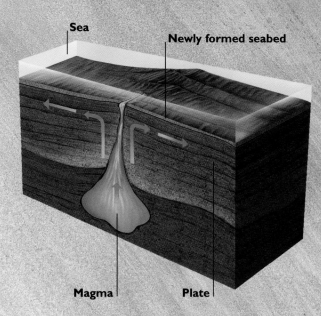

Sea
Newly formed seabed
Magma
Plate

Spreading ridge

At a spreading ridge, two plates are pushed apart as magma rises out of the Earth's crust and hardens.

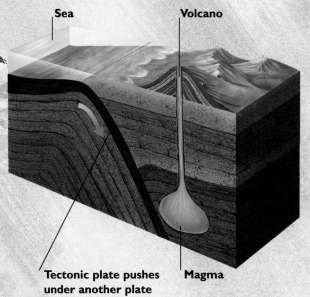

Sea
Volcano
Tectonic plate pushes under another plate
Magma

Subduction zone

At a subduction zone, one plate pushes beneath another and melts into new magma. Volcanoes are most common along the tectonic plate boundaries on land and at sea.

Fiery beginnings

Billions of years ago, when the Earth was newly formed, volcanoes were more common than they are now. Huge volcanic eruptions created many of the mountains and landscapes that we know today.

New islands

On 14 November 1963, a cook on board a fishing boat near Iceland spotted a distant column of smoke rising from the sea. Thinking another boat must be on fire, the crew steered towards it – only to find that the smoke was churning out of the sea itself. Just below the water surface, an undersea volcano was erupting with a series of violent explosions. Later that day, rock and ash from the eruption had piled up high enough to be seen above the sea surface, and a brand-new island was born.

Surtsey is born

The Icelanders named the new island Surtsey ('Surtr's island'), after Surtr, a fire giant from Norse mythology. In its early days, Surtsey was built of rocks and ash which piled up around several craters in a series of volcanic explosions. The explosions happened because sea water seeped into the volcano's vents, forming steam and causing a build-up of pressure. After Surtsey grew higher, the crater vents rose clear of the sea and its eruptions calmed down.

Scientists on Surtsey

As soon as news of Surtsey's appearance spread, volcano scientists from around the world rushed to Iceland to witness a volcano being born out of the sea. Later, biologists and ecologists also went to Surtsey to study the way living things took up residence on the new island.

Ridges and hotspots

Surtsey formed on the Mid-Atlantic Ridge (see page 23), where magma constantly breaks through the sea floor. If a volcano on an undersea ridge grows very large, or is in shallow water, it can break the water surface to form new land. Volcanic islands can also form far away from plate boundaries, at hotspots – isolated areas of active magma in the middle of the Earth's plates.

Hello Hawaii

The chain of islands that make up Hawaii were built on a hotspot. A volcano formed on the seabed over the hotspot and eventually broke through the sea surface to form an island. Over time, the plate Hawaii is on gradually moved, while the hotspot stayed in the same place. Each new eruption created a new Hawaiian island, resulting in a string of islands.

Boom!
An ash cloud erupts from the sea next to Surtsey in 1965, two years after the island first formed.

Empty island
Surtsey is uninhabited except by visiting scientists. These scientists are measuring plant growth on the cooled lava.

Surtr, god of fire
In Norse mythology, Surtr was the leader of the fire giants. He carried a flaming sword with which he planned to set fire to the whole world.

Treasure troves

When 15-year-old Erasmus Jacobs found a strange white rock on his father's farm one day in 1866, he had little idea his discovery would make his country, South Africa, rich. What he had found was a huge diamond, carried out of the Earth by a volcano.

Rock factories

Volcanoes create rocks and minerals in two main ways. The magma and lava in a volcano is made of molten rock. It cools and hardens into different types of rock, such as hard, black basalt; light, rough-textured pumice; and tough, grainy granite. These types of rocks, formed from lava, are called igneous (meaning 'fiery') rocks.

Rocky pinnacles
These rock formations sticking up out of the ground at the Pinnacles National Monument, California, USA, were created by an ancient volcano.

Changing rocks

Volcanoes can also change existing rocks by subjecting them to massive heat and pressure. For example, limestone rock in the ground near a volcanic vent can change into a different rock, marble, if it is heated and squeezed by hot underground magma. Rocks created in this way are called metamorphic rocks.

Underground search

Miners make their way through a tunnel in a diamond mine near Pretoria, South Africa, searching for diamonds trapped in the rock.

The Earth's riches

Diamonds are formed in magma beneath the Earth's crust, and get trapped in rocks such as kimberlite that are created when volcanoes erupt. Volcanoes give us not just diamonds but many precious stones, such as obsidian and peridot, and useful rocks and minerals. Pumice is a rock made from lava that contains bubbles of gas. When the lava cools, the bubbles are trapped in the rock, making pumice very light. Because of its texture, for thousands of years people have used pumice to rub away rough skin.

Black sand beach

Some volcanic islands, such as Hawaii and Iceland, have black beaches. They are made from basalt – an igneous rock formed when lava cools – that has been broken down into sand particles by the action of the waves.

Starting again

When a big volcano erupts, it can change
the land around it for years to come.
A thick covering of dust and ash swamps
plant life and chokes the soil. Pyroclastic
flows destroy even the biggest trees, and
a layer of cooled, hardened lava covers the
land in bare rock. The empty, barren waste
can take decades to return to normal.

Fertile farming

Highly volcanic areas have some of the most fertile
farmland in the world. This crop of rice is growing
in Bali, Indonesia, in the shadow of a volcano.

Coming back to life

First, simple plants such as mosses and lichens grow
from spores carried on the wind. Insects and birds
arrive to feed on these plants. Bird droppings, plant
matter and crumbling rock particles then build a layer
of soil, where bigger plants and trees can grow. As soil
gradually gathers, it collects in folds and cracks in the
rocks, and small plants can begin to put down roots.
Plant leaves, fruits and seeds provide food for animals,
so once plants are established, more animals can arrive.

Bringing fertility

Volcanic eruptions are often disastrous for farmers. Lava flows, lahars, poisonous gases or a thick layer of ash can destroy crops, make fields unusable and ruin a lifetime's work. A lighter sprinkling of ash, though, is a different story. Volcanic ash often contains minerals such as potassium and phosphorus, which plants thrive on.

Precious land

Farmland around volcanoes is incredibly fertile. It can grow bumper crops of produce such as onions, citrus fruits, olives, and grapes for winemaking, which are often renowned for their rich flavours. Even a large, damaging eruption will eventually leave the land more fertile. This is one reason why people often choose to live and farm near active volcanoes, despite the dangers. In 2004, the kingdom of Jordan even gave the USA's President Bush a state gift of six jars of volcanic soil, showing how highly it is valued.

After the eruption

Life slowly returns to the volcanic rock around a volcano. Lichen grows on the rocks and soil begins to collect in crevices, allowing grasses and small plants to take hold and thrive.

Soil recipe

Soil is made up of bits of rock, along with plant and animal matter. After a volcanic eruption, the basic ingredients for soil gradually build up.

VOLCANOES AND PEOPLE

For as long as they have been erupting, volcanoes have been important to the people who live near them. With their sudden explosions, roaring, booming and flinging of fire and rock, it is no surprise that many early peoples thought volcanoes were mighty gods. Others believed they were where the gods lived. In Greek mythology, the great god of fire Hephaestus used a volcano as a forge to make weapons. In Hawaii, the volcano goddess Pelé was said to start volcanic eruptions when she was angry, by digging in the ground with a magical stick. Japan's Mount Fuji is the traditional home of the Shinto goddess Konohana Sakuya Hime.

Holy mountain
The volcano Mount Fuji in Japan is sacred to followers of the Shinto religion.

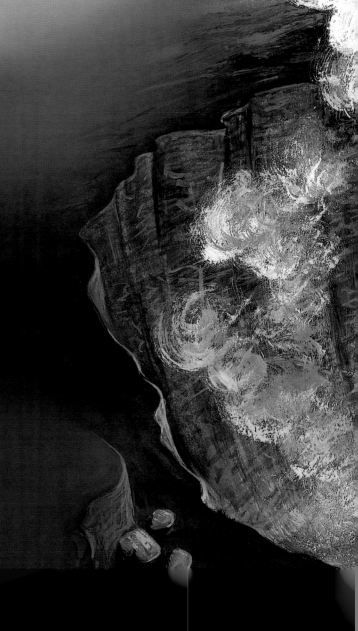

God of fire
The ancient Greeks believed Hephaestus had a forge under a volcano where he used the fire to make weapons and armour. His Roman name was Vulcan. The word volcano comes from Vulcan.

Ancient stories

For thousands of years, humans have created myths and legends as explanations for natural events, and there are many old stories about volcanoes. The ancient Greeks told how Prometheus stole fire from Hephaestus's volcano and gave it to humans. The myth of the lost city of Atlantis sinking beneath the waves may be based on the Greek island of Santorini, which exploded and collapsed into the sea in ancient times. And in the volcanic region of Kamchatka in northeastern Russia, people used to believe that giant demons lived on the tops of the volcanoes. At night it was thought the demons went down to the sea to catch fish, then cooked them – which is why the volcanoes glowed with fire.

Human sacrifice

According to local legend, people used to throw young girls into the fiery crater of the Masaya volcano in Nicaragua. They were hoping to appease the fire goddess Chaciutique, so that she would stop the volcano erupting.

Living with volcanoes

Around the world, more than 300 million people – nearly one in 20 of the Earth's population – live in the shadow of active volcanoes, where they are at risk from eruptions. Mount Vesuvius in Italy, Mount Rainier in the USA and Popocatépetl in Mexico are just three volcanoes in highly populated areas that could erupt at any time. So why do people stay near volcanoes? There are two main reasons. First, fertile volcanic soil makes good farming land, which provides a living for millions of people. Second, poverty and overcrowding mean that for many people living near volcanoes, it is impossible to leave.

After an eruption

When Mount Pinatubo in the Philippines erupted in 1991, many people lost their homes and farms. About 700 people died in the tragedy, but many more lives were saved. Because scientists were able to predict when the eruption would take place, people had time to leave the danger zone and the government moved nearly 70,000 people to safety.

Being prepared

Scientists are learning more and more about how to predict a volcanic eruption (see page 50) and modern technology, such as satellite imaging, makes it much easier to see what is happening on remote volcanic mountaintops. If an eruption is predicted, the best course of action is to evacuate the area as soon as possible. When a volcano erupts, anyone left behind might be able to protect themselves by staying indoors and avoiding river valleys and low-lying areas where poisonous gas or mudflows could be headed.

Town under fire

Eldfell is a volcano on the Icelandic island of Heimaey. When it erupted in 1973, lava flows threatened to engulf the town of Vestmannaeyjar. The town was evacuated, but some of the islanders stayed to battle with the lava, spraying it with seawater (left) to cool it and keep it away from the houses. They succeeded in saving a large part of the town, though dozens of homes were lost.

Volcano power

In some volcanic areas, such as Iceland, heat energy from magma under the ground can be used to heat water and run power stations. Water is pumped into the ground, where magma heats it up. The hot water returns to the surface and is used to make steam. The steam is used to drive turbines and generate electricity. This kind of energy is called 'geothermal' (meaning 'Earth-heat') energy.

On the surface, the heat energy is used to make steam, which drives turbines, generating electricity.

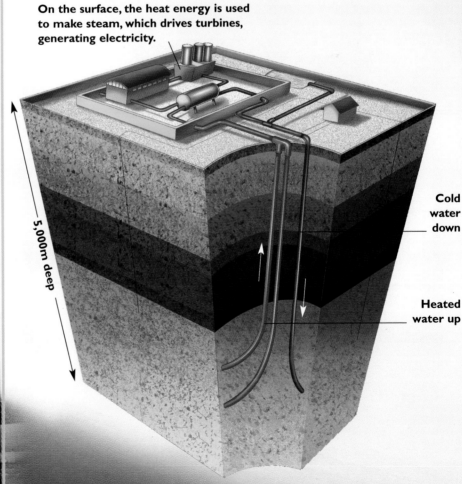

5,000m deep

Cold water down

Heated water up

Visiting volcanoes

In 1993, a group of scientists and tourists was exploring the crater of the Galeras volcano in Colombia when it suddenly erupted. Six scientists and three tourists were killed. Getting close to volcanoes can be risky, yet we find them fascinating – there are few sights more exciting than a volcano in action. Every day, thousands of tourists visit active volcanoes. At many volcano sites you can go right up to the crater. These include Poas in Costa Rica, Kilauea in Hawaii, Bromo in Indonesia, Mutnovsky in Russia and Vesuvius in Italy. Usually they are very closely checked and monitored, and closed to the public at the first sign of a major eruption.

Old Faithful

Old Faithful is a geyser in Yellowstone National Park in the USA. This natural hot water fountain is caused by magma heating up underground water. As the water gets hotter, steam builds up under pressure, and eventually forces a jet of water out of the ground. Old Faithful goes off every 60–90 minutes, for about three minutes at a time.

Hot spring spas

Hot springs often occur near volcanoes, where water heated by underground magma flows out of the ground. The water often contains dissolved volcanic minerals that are thought to be good for the skin. This is the Blue Lagoon, a hot spring spa in Iceland.

Safe to see

Volcanic areas often contain amazing water features, such as geysers, bubbling mud pools and mineral lakes, which tourists can visit safely. Some have volcanic spas where naturally hot, volcanic springs are deliberately diverted to fill swimming pools. Or tourists can view a spectacular volcano from a distance, by taking a helicopter flight over and around it. Running tourist attractions is one way for people who live in volcanic regions to make a living.

On the edge

These tourists are looking into the crater of Volcan Poas in Costa Rica, which contains a mineral-rich lake.

From the air

A trip in a helicopter or light aircraft around a volcano is an exciting but safe way to watch an eruption at close range. People in this helicopter are watching an eruption of Mount Kilauea, a volcano in the Hawaii Volcanoes National Park.

Scream sunset
Edvard Munch's famous painting *The Scream* is thought to show a volcanic sunset caused by the eruption of Krakatau in Indonesia in 1883. The blood-red sunsets could be seen as far away as Norway, where Munch lived.

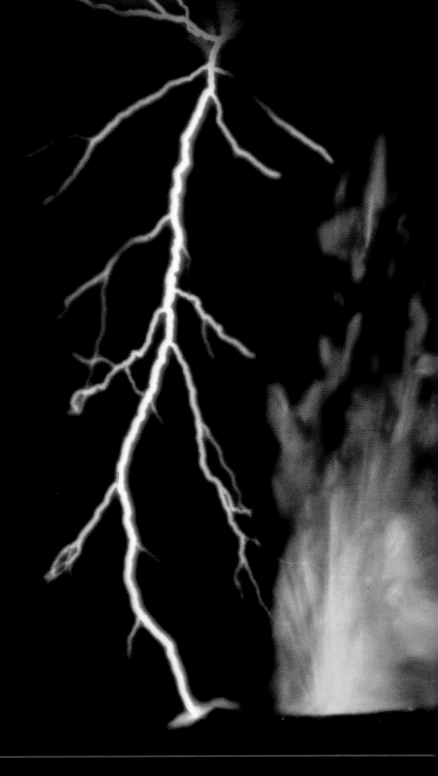

Lightning and fire
During an eruption, a violent lightning storm rages over the summit of the Japanese volcano Sakurajima.

Volcanic weather

When Paricutín in Mexico was erupting, from 1943 to 1952, not a single person was killed by ash, rocks, lava, gases or mudflows. But three people did die from being struck by volcanic lightning. Many volcanoes seem to create a massive lightning storm directly above the crater as they erupt. Scientists are not sure why, but this could be caused by ash, dust or water particles released from magma rubbing together and building up an electrical charge. This is just one of the ways in which volcanoes can change the weather.

Red sky at night

Volcanic dust scattered through the atmosphere is sometimes called a volcanic haze. As well as creating red sunsets, a haze can give people breathing problems.

Global cooling

The eruption of Mount Tambora (above) in Indonesia in 1815 was the most violent explosive eruption in modern history, releasing four times as much energy as Krakatau. The ash and dust it threw into the sky caused temperatures to drop around the world, and the following year, 1816, became known as 'The Year Without a Summer'.

World weather effects

Volcanic lightning only happens very near an erupting volcano, but other volcanic weather can affect a huge area, or even the whole planet. A really big eruption, such as that of Mount St Helens in 1980, throws so much ash and dust into the sky that it blocks out the Sun over a large area, making day seem like night. As the dust spreads out and floats higher into the atmosphere, it changes the way the Sun's light is scattered, leading to amazing bright red sunsets. Volcanic dust in the atmosphere also combines with water to make droplets of acid which absorb and reflect sunlight, so that less heat and light reach the Earth.

STUDYING VOLCANOES

In 1991, volcanologists Katia and Maurice Krafft went to Japan to study and film an eruption of Mount Unzen. As they watched a pyroclastic flow surge down the mountain, the flow suddenly changed direction. The Kraffts, another volcanologist named Harry Glicken, and 40 journalists were killed. Working with volcanoes can be extremely dangerous. But volcanology is also exciting, adventurous and very important.

Analyzing volcanoes

Like other scientists, volcanologists spend most of their time in the laboratory. They analyze samples of lava, rock, mud and gas from volcanoes. They also study old layers of lava on volcanoes to try to find out when a volcano erupted in the past, and when and how it could erupt again. About a fifth of a volcanologist's time, though, is spent visiting volcanoes to carry out fieldwork. This includes mapping old mudflows and lava flows, measuring changes in the Earth that might predict an eruption and, most daring of all, collecting hot lava, ash and volcanic gases from erupting volcanoes.

Sulphur samples

This volcanologist is collecting sulphur deposits on the active volcano Mutnovsky in Kamchatka, Russia. Sulphur can form where sulphurous volcanic gases escape from craters and cracks on volcanoes.

48

Collecting lava
A scientist uses a special lava ladle to collect lava samples during an eruption of Kilauea in Hawaii.

Safety suit
Volcanologists sometimes have to work near lava flows where the heat is intense. A safety suit like the one shown below, covered in a silver coating, reflects heat away from the body and helps the scientist to stay cool.

Predicting the future

Volcanologists can predict volcanic activity, which means that people living near a volcano can be warned of an eruption and escape in time. Luckily, most volcanoes give some warnings before a big eruption, such as a series of smaller eruptions before the main one. Other signs are more difficult to see or hear, so volcanologists use special equipment to detect the changes that show a big blast is on the way. They can also study a volcano's past, known as its 'eruptive history', to find out when an eruption is likely to happen again.

Volcano observatory

When a volcano erupts constantly, volcanologists need to observe it all the time. Sometimes they build permanent observatories near volcanoes, where they can stay full-time. This is the Montserrat Volcano Observatory, which monitors the Soufriere Hills volcano on the Caribbean island of Montserrat.

Measuring the Earth

A geodimeter measures the Earth's shape by sending out a laser beam that bounces off a receiver set up some distance away. By taking the same measurement many times, volcanologists can see if the time the beam of light takes to bounce back is changing. If it is, this means that the distance is changing and so the Earth's shape is changing, too.

Eruptions over time

The timeline below shows the eruptions of the dormant volcano Snaefellsjökull, in Iceland. Volcanologists can calculate the history of a volcano from the layers of lava and ash around it. This may help to predict the next eruption.

8460BCE

6050BCE

4550B

10000BCE

Eruption clues

There are several different clues volcanologists use to predict eruptions. First, they study the shape of the ground, as magma gathering under pressure inside a volcano can make the ground bulge and crack. They use tiltmeters, which can detect the ground tilting, and geodimeters, which use lasers to sense changes in the Earth's shape. Second, they measure how much gas a volcano is releasing. Volcanoes usually give off more gas just before an eruption as the magma inside them pushes upwards. As with earthquakes, scientists use seismometers to pick up earth tremors, because magma squeezing between solid rocks inside a volcano can make the ground shake.

Lava walking

Volcanologists often need to walk on or near freshly erupted lava as they explore active volcanoes. Sometimes a lava flow cools on the top, but stays molten underneath, creating a solid 'roof' that can support a person's weight.

Volcanology long ago

Volcanology is not a new science. The ancient Greeks and Romans studied volcanoes and the Italian scientist Lazzaro Spallanzani (1729–99, below) made detailed studies of Mount Etna, measuring lava temperatures and analyzing volcanic gases.

4050BCE	2970BCE	2400BCE	2010BCE	1000BCE	200CE

2270BCE

Today

51

Supervolcano!

What wiped out the dinosaurs? Some say it was an asteroid hitting the Earth around 65 million years ago, throwing up dust and debris into the atmosphere and blocking out the Sun. Recently, though, some scientists have started to think something else could have been responsible – a supervolcano. This is an enormous volcanic eruption, far bigger than any in recorded history. Studies of ancient lava flows show that these huge eruptions did happen in prehistoric times, and could happen again. In a supervolcano, a vast magma chamber explodes out of the ground, releasing far more lava, ash and rock than the biggest eruptions of modern times.

Ready to blow

Yellowstone National Park, in north-western USA, sits on the site of an ancient supervolcano. It erupted about two million years ago, 1.3 million years ago and 640,000 years ago. If it follows the same pattern, another eruption is due around now. The previous eruptions were so big, they covered most of what is now the USA in lava and ash.

Supervolcano size

A supervolcano would release at least 1,000km^3 of volcanic material – six times more than the biggest eruption in modern history. The biggest prehistoric supervolcanoes threw out as much as 1,000,000km^3 of rocks and other material. Supervolcanoes do not form mountains. So much magma is blasted out of the Earth that they leave bowl-shaped calderas. The edge of the huge caldera at Yellowstone Park is easy to see today.

Dinosaur disaster

A supervolcano eruption could have killed the dinosaurs by filling the sky with dark ash and smoke. With sunlight unable to get through, plants would have died and the Earth's temperature would have dropped. Many animals would have run out of food. Others could have been killed by lava, poisonous gases and pyroclastic flows.

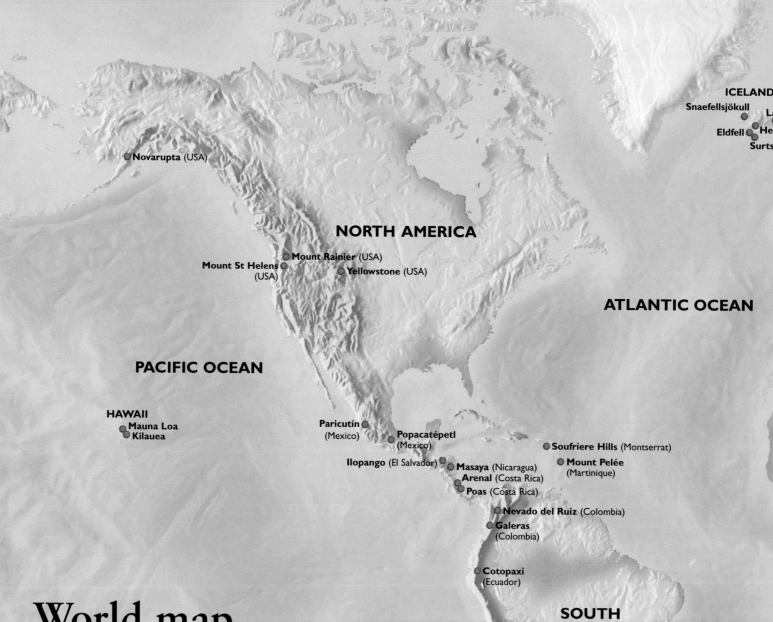

ICELAND
Snaefellsjökull · Laki
Eldfell · Hekla
Surtsey

Novarupta (USA)

NORTH AMERICA

Mount Rainier (USA)
Mount St Helens (USA)
Yellowstone (USA)

ATLANTIC OCEAN

PACIFIC OCEAN

HAWAII
Mauna Loa
Kilauea

Paricutín (Mexico)
Popacatépetl (Mexico)
Soufriere Hills (Montserrat)
Ilopango (El Salvador)
Masaya (Nicaragua)
Mount Pelée (Martinique)
Arenal (Costa Rica)
Poas (Costa Rica)
Nevado del Ruiz (Colombia)
Galeras (Colombia)
Cotopaxi (Ecuador)

SOUTH AMERICA

World map of volcanoes

This map shows the world's best-known volcanoes, including all the volcanoes mentioned in this book. You can see that many of them are found in the countries that lie around the Pacific Ocean. This circle of volcanoes is known as the 'Ring of Fire'. Volcanoes are often found on small islands too, where volcanic activity on the seabed has caused an island to form.

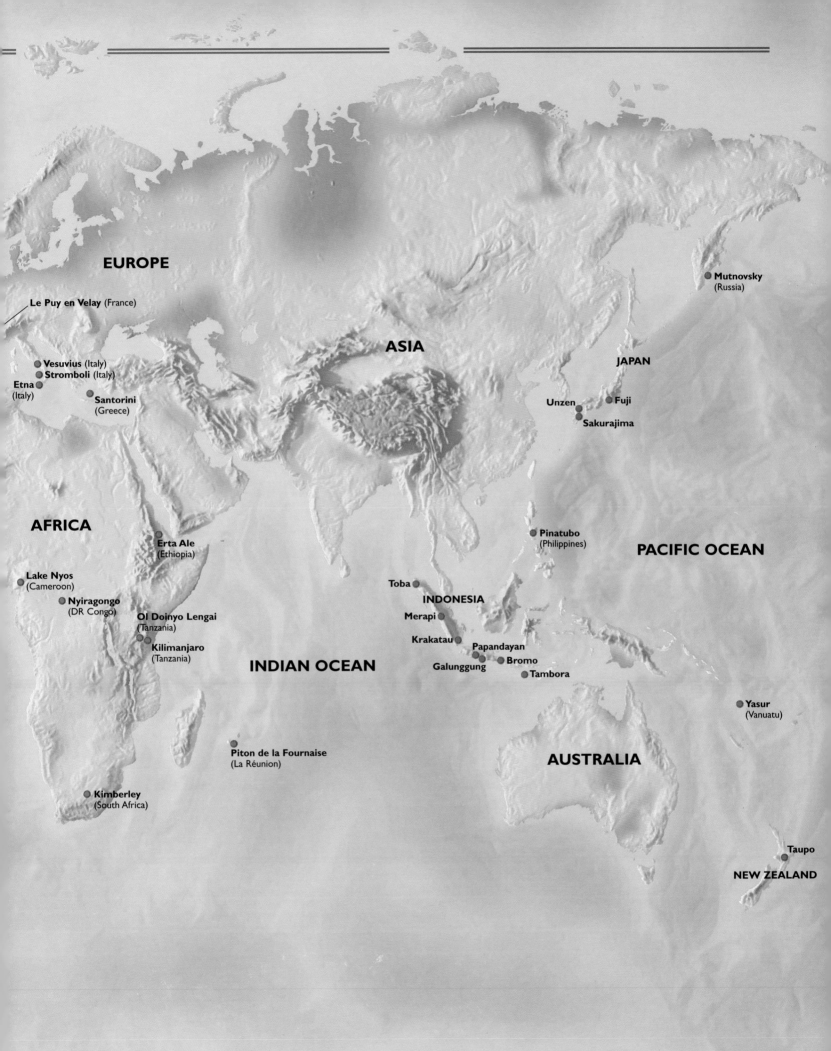

EUROPE

Le Puy en Velay (France)

Vesuvius (Italy)
Stromboli (Italy)
Etna (Italy)
Santorini (Greece)

ASIA

JAPAN

Mutnovsky (Russia)

Unzen
Fuji
Sakurajima

AFRICA

Erta Ale (Ethiopia)

Lake Nyos (Cameroon)
Nyiragongo (DR Congo)
Ol Doinyo Lengai (Tanzania)
Kilimanjaro (Tanzania)

Pinatubo (Philippines)

PACIFIC OCEAN

Toba
INDONESIA
Merapi
Krakatau
Papandayan
Galunggung
Bromo
Tambora

INDIAN OCEAN

Piton de la Fournaise (La Réunion)

AUSTRALIA

Yasur (Vanuatu)

Kimberley (South Africa)

Taupo

NEW ZEALAND

ANTARCTICA

55

ERUPTION TIMELINE

This timeline lists some of the most famous and destructive volcanic eruptions and events ever known.

Date	Volcano	Description
c. 640000BCE	Yellowstone, USA	The most recent eruption of the supervolcano under what is now Yellowstone National Park covered most of North America with volcanic ash.
c. 70000BCE	Toba, Indonesia	The biggest volcanic eruption of the last two million years, this supervolcano released 2,800km^3 of volcanic material.
c. 1630BCE	Santorini, Greece	The Greek island of Santorini (also called Thera) was blown apart by a huge volcanic eruption, leaving a caldera. Thousands of people were probably killed.
79CE	Vesuvius, Italy	Massive Plinian-type eruption destroyed the towns of Pompeii and Herculaneum with pyroclastic flows, killing at least 3,500 people.
1006	Mount Merapi, Indonesia	The major eruption devastated the island of Java, leading to the downfall of its ancient Hindu kingdom.
1631	Vesuvius, Italy	Another eruption of Vesuvius released lava flows and mudflows that claimed up to 3,500 lives.
1766	Hekla, Iceland	Iceland's biggest lava flow in history wiped out thousands of farm animals.
1772	Papandayan, Indonesia	The volcano collapsed in on itself, releasing ash and debris that killed almost 3,000 people.
1783	Laki, Iceland	Lava flows and deadly gases destroyed farmland and livestock, leading to a famine that killed at least 9,000 people.
1792	Unzen, Japan	In Japan's worst-ever volcanic disaster, part of this volcano collapsed, causing a tsunami that killed up to 15,000 people.
1815	Tambora, Indonesia	The biggest, most violent eruption known in modern times. Over 90,000 people died in pyroclastic flows and later from starvation and disease.
1822	Galunggung, Indonesia	Hot mudflows from this eruption claimed around 4,000 lives.
1883	Krakatau, Indonesia	Explosive eruption blasted the island of Krakatau to pieces, creating deadly tsunamis and turning skies red around the world. The death toll was around 36,000.

1902	Mount Pelée, Martinique	A pyroclastic flow laden with burning gas from the erupting volcano enveloped the town of St Pierre, killing 28,000 people.
1919	Kelut, Indonesia	Hot mudflows from an eruption killed around 5,000 people.
1943	Paricutín, Mexico	A brand-new volcano grew from nothing after a crack appeared in a cornfield and began spewing out smoke, lava and ash.
1951	Lamington, Papua New Guinea	Pyroclastic flows and choking dust from this volcano killed more than 3,000 people.
1963	Surtsey, Iceland	An undersea eruption broke through the water surface and created a new island.
1973	Eldfell, Iceland	This island eruption damaged the town of Vestmannaeyjar, but few were hurt.
1980	Mount St Helens, USA	A giant explosive eruption blew one side of the volcano away, and pyroclastic flows and ashfalls flattened huge areas of forest. Fifty-seven people died.
1983	Kilauea, Hawaii	Kilauea began a long eruption that is continuing to this day.
1985	Nevado del Ruiz, Colombia	Around 23,000 people were killed when a massive mudflow formed during an eruption, swept down a river valley and swamped the town of Armero.
1986	Lake Nyos, Cameroon	A huge cloud of carbon dioxide gas released from this volcanic lake suffocated more than 1,700 people to death in the village of Lower Nyos.
1989	Kilauea, Hawaii	Lava from Kilauea ruined a volcano visitors' centre and 45 homes on Hawaii.
1991	Pinatubo, Philippines	Warning systems and evacuations saved many thousands from this hugely violent eruption, though around 700 people were killed by mudflows and from homes collapsing under the weight of volcanic ash that fell on them.
1991	Unzen, Japan	During an eruption, a pyroclastic flow changed course and swept away 43 people, including three volcanologists.
1993	Galeras, Colombia	A sudden eruption took visiting scientists and tourists by surprise, killing nine people.
1997	Soufriere Hills, Montserrat	A large eruption killed 20 people and destroyed the island's airport.
2002	Nyiragongo, Democratic Republic of Congo	Lava flows from this eruption killed only 45 people, but left 120,000 homeless.

RECORDS AND FACTS

The Volcanic Explosivity Index

A way of measuring a volcanic eruption, the Volcanic Explosivity Index, or VEI, takes into account a number of different factors, such as how violently the volcano explodes, how much volcanic material it throws out, how often it erupts and how high its plume of smoke and ash rises into the sky. The VEI scale, invented in 1982 by volcanologists Chris Newhall and Steve Self, has nine categories ranging from 0 to 8 (it can be extended to go higher if necessary). This chart shows how it works.

VEI	Description	Plume height	Volume of material	Eruption frequency	Volcano example
0	Non-explosive	Up to 100m	$1,000m^3$	Daily	Kilauea
1	Gentle	100–1,000m	$10,000m^3$	Daily	Stromboli
2	Explosive	1–5km	$1,000,000m^3$	Weekly	Galeras, 1993
3	Severe	3–15km	$10,000,000m^3$	Yearly	Nevado del Ruiz, 1985
4	Cataclysmic	10–25km	$0.1km^3$	Every 10 years	Galunggung, 1822
5	Paroxysmal	Over 25km	$1km^3$	Every 50 years	Mount St Helens, 1980
6	Colossal	Over 25km	$10km^3$	Every 100 years	Krakatoa, 1883
7	Super-colossal	Over 25km	$100km^3$	Every 1,000 years	Tambora, 1815
8	Mega-colossal	Over 25km	$1,000km^3$	Every 10,000 years	Toba, 70000BCE

The biggest eruptions

There were many massive and supervolcanic eruptions in prehistoric times, but we are not sure how big they all were, so this list shows the biggest volcanic eruptions in recorded history. Volcanic eruptions are hard to measure, so different sources may give slightly different lists.

Volcano	Date	Km³ of material	VEI
Tambora, Indonesia	1815	150	7
Taupo, New Zealand	181CE	100	7
Santorini, Greece	1630BCE	60	7
Krakatau, Indonesia	1883	25	6
Laki, Iceland	1783	25	6
Ilopango, El Salvador	260CE	20	6
Novarupta, USA	1912	15	6
Pinatubo, Philippines	1991	10	6
Vesuvius, Italy	79CE	3	5
Mount St Helens, USA	1980	0.7	5

The deadliest eruptions

The deadliest ever volcanic eruptions are not always the same as the biggest eruptions, because the number of people a volcano kills depends on how many people live near it and how it erupts. Deadly volcanoes are the most famous volcanoes because they are the ones that make news stories.

Volcano	Date	Death toll	Deadly effects
Tambora, Indonesia	1815	90,000	Starvation
Krakatau, Indonesia	1883	36,000	Tsunamis
Mount Pelée, Martinique	1902	28,000	Pyroclastic flows
Nevado del Ruiz, Colombia	1985	23,000	Mudflows
Unzen, Japan	1792	15,000	Tsunami
Laki, Iceland	1783	9,000	Starvation
Kelut, Indonesia	1919	5,000	Mudflows
Galunggung, Indonesia	1822	4,000	Mudflows
Vesuvius, Italy	79CE	3,500	Pyroclastic flows
Vesuvius, Italy	1631	3,500	Mud and lava

Most active volcanoes

The most active volcanoes in the world are those that erupt most often and produce the most lava and other volcanic material. Scientists do not always agree on which volcanoes are the most active and this list can change regularly.

Arenal, Costa Rica
Erta Ale, Ethiopia
Etna, Italy
Kilauea, Hawaii
Merapi, Indonesia
Ol Doinyo Lengai, Tanzania
Piton de la Fournaise, La Réunion
Stromboli, Italy
Unzen, Japan
Yasur, Vanuatu

Most volcanic countries

The countries listed below are among the most volcanic in the world, meaning they have the most, biggest and most active volcanoes. Each country is shown with a selection of its most famous volcanoes.

Colombia	Galeras; Nevado del Ruiz
Costa Rica	Arenal; Irazu; Poas
Iceland	Eldafell; Hekla; Laki
Indonesia	Krakatau; Merapi; Tambora
Italy	Etna; Stromboli; Vesuvius
Japan	Fuji; Unzen
Mexico	Paricutín; Popacatépetl
Philippines	Mayon; Pinatubo
USA (mainland)	Mount Rainier; Mount St Helens
USA (Hawaii)	Kilauea; Mauna Loa

Glossary

This glossary explains some of the words used in this book and in other books about volcanoes.

'a'a A kind of lava that cracks and folds over as it cools, making rock with a rough surface.

active volcano A volcano that is erupting or has erupted within the last few hundred years.

archaeologist An expert who studies old ruins and objects to find out about past peoples and events.

ash Volcanic ash is made from lava that cools and shatters as it is hurled into the air.

ash plume The column of ash, smoke and dust that rises into the air from an erupting volcano.

bomb A chunk of solid rock thrown out of an erupting volcano.

block A lump of semi-molten lava thrown through the air from an erupting volcano.

caldera A ring-shaped hollow formed by a volcano collapsing. Calderas are often filled with water.

cinder cone A volcano with a triangular shape and a wide crater, created by Strombolian-type eruptions.

crater A wide, usually circular, bowl-shaped opening at the top of a volcano's vent, where lava is thrown out of a volcano.

dormant volcano A volcano that has not erupted within the last few hundred years, but could erupt again.

dyke A smaller vent, leading from the main vent to the side of a volcano.

eruptive history The record of all the eruptions of a particular volcano through its lifetime.

extinct volcano A volcano that has stopped erupting and is not expected to erupt again.

extrusive igneous rock Igneous rock that forms when lava cools after flowing out of a volcano onto the Earth's surface.

fertile Fertile soil is soil that is rich and very good for growing crops.

fieldwork Scientific study that is done in the outside world, for example on an active volcano, instead of in the science laboratory.

fissure A crack in the ground where volcanic gases or lava can escape.

flanks The slopes of a volcano.

fumarole A jet of steam that escapes from a crack in the ground, carrying volcanic gases with it.

geodimeter A device that uses lasers to detect changes in the shape of the ground.

geothermal energy Heat energy from inside the Earth, which can be used to run power stations or heat homes.

geyser A jet of hot water and steam that shoots out of the ground periodically. Geysers are found in volcanic areas where magma heats up underground water.

Hawaiian-type eruption A gentle eruption in which runny lava flows down the volcano's sides.

hotspot An isolated area of hot, liquid magma under the Earth's crust, which can create volcanoes away from plate boundaries.

igneous rock Rock created when magma or lava cools and hardens.

intrusive igneous rock Igneous rock that forms when magma cools underground inside a volcano, without reaching the surface.

lahar A river of mud that forms when volcanic ash combines with rain, melted ice or river water.

lava Molten rock that flows out of a volcano.

magma Molten rock inside the Earth.

magma chamber A large area underneath a volcano where magma builds up before an eruption.

metamorphic rock Rock that is created when heat and pressure inside a volcano change existing rocks into other types of rock.

mudflow A river of mud that flows down the side of a volcano after an eruption. Also called a lahar.

observatory A building or station where scientists go to watch something, such as the stars or a volcano.

pahoehoe A type of lava that cools to form smooth, rope-like rock.

parasitic cone A small mini-volcano that forms where lava erupts out of a dyke on the side of a volcano.

pillow lava Lava that cools underwater, forming pillow-shaped lumps.

pipe A tube carrying magma from a magma chamber up inside a volcano.

plate boundary An area where the edges of two or more tectonic plates meet, and where most earthquakes and volcanoes are found.

Plinian-type eruption A violent, explosive eruption caused by a build-up of thick, sticky lava.

pyroclastic flow A fast-moving surge of rocks, gases and volcanic ash released by some types of very violent volcanic eruptions.

seamount A mountain under the sea. Many seamounts are created by volcanic eruptions on the seabed.

seismometer A device that detects tremors and vibrations in the Earth's crust.

shield volcano A volcano with a wide, flat shape, created by runny lava spreading out over a wide area.

spreading ridge A plate boundary where magma rises out of the Earth between two tectonic plates, pushing them apart and creating new sections of the Earth's crust.

stratovolcano A tall volcano with a pointed tip, created by explosive eruptions of sticky lava.

Strombolian-type eruption A volcanic eruption in which lumps of lava fly upwards out of the volcano's crater.

subduction zone A plate boundary where one tectonic plate is pushed beneath another.

supervolcano A very big volcanic eruption, bigger than any in recent history, that releases 1,000 km³ or more of volcanic material.

tectonic plates The huge sections of rock that fit together to make up the Earth's crust.

tephra Solid volcanic material ejected from an erupting volcano, such as ash, rocks and dust.

tiltmeter A device that can detect changes in the angle of the ground's surface.

tremor A shaking or vibrating of the Earth, which often occurs shortly before a volcano erupts.

tsunami A huge wave that can be caused by a volcanic eruption at or below sea level.

vent A tube carrying magma from inside a volcano to the surface, where it flows out as lava.

Volcanic Explosivity Index (VEI) A scale designed to measure and categorize volcanic eruptions by their size, violence and frequency.

volcanic haze Dust and ash that collect in the atmosphere after a big volcanic eruption.

volcanic lightning Lightning that forms directly above an erupting volcano.

volcanic plug An tower of cooled, hardened lava from the inside of an ancient volcano that has mostly worn away.

volcanology The science of volcanoes.

volcanologist Someone who studies volcanoes.

Index

Further reading

Books

My Best Book of Volcanoes by Simon Adams,
  Kingfisher, 2002

Volcano and Earthquake (Eyewitness series)
  by Susanna Van Rose, Dorling Kindersley, 2002

Violent Volcanoes (Horrible Geography series)
  by Anita Ganeri, Scholastic Hippo, 1999

Earthquakes and Volcanoes (Looking at Landscapes
  series) by Alison Rae, Evans Brothers, 2005

Websites

VolcanoWorld:
  http://volcano.und.edu/

How volcanoes work:
www.geology.sdsu.edu/how_volcanoes_work/

Global Volcanism Program:
www.volcano.si.edu/index.cfm

Supervolcano:
www.bbc.co.uk/sn/tvradio/programmes/supervolcano/
  index.shtml

Savage Earth volcano animation:
www.pbs.org/wnet/savageearth/animations/volcanoes/
  main.html

Listen to a volcano:
http://kiska.giseis.alaska.edu/Input/celso/sounds/
  soundtest.html

Acknowledgements

The publisher would like to thank the following for permission to reproduce their material. Every care has been taken to trace copyright holders. However, if there have been unintentional omissions or failure to trace copyright holders, we apologize and will, if informed, endeavour to make corrections in any future edition.

The publisher would like to thank the following for supplying photographs for this book:

b = bottom, c = centre, l = left, r = right, t = top

Pages: **4**tl, **11**tr, **11**cr, **17**tr, **30**tr, **31**cr, **49**tl, **50**br, **51**tr: U. S. Geological Survey;
4tr: Yann Arthus-Bertrand/corbis;
5c: Mosista Pambudi/shutterstock;
6tr: Bychkov Kirill Alexandrovich/shutterstock;
6b: Douglas Peebles/corbis;
8–9tc: Roger Ressmeyer/corbis;
9br: Bembaron Jeremy/corbis sygma;
12–13b: Larry Dale Gordon/zefa/corbis;
13tc: Tashka/dreamstime.com;
14–15b: Anders Ryman/corbis;
15tr NOAA (National Oceanic & Atmospheric Administration);
16–17b: Sergio Dorantes/corbis;
18–19b: Index Stock Imagery/photolibrary;
18bl: Bart Parren/shutterstock; **19**br: Albo/shutterstock;
22–23c: Yann Arthus-Bertrand/corbis;
23tr: Colin Palmer Photography/alamy;
24–25b: Jacques Langevin/corbis sygma;
25br: Jacques Langevin/corbis sygma;
26bl: Michael Maslan Historic Photographs/corbis;
27tr: Wendy Kaveney Photography/shutterstock;
29tr: Rykoff Collection/corbis; **29**br: Peter Turnley/corbis;
34–35bl: Science Photo Library/photolibrary;
35tr: Bob Krist/corbis; **36–37**bl: Michael Almond/shutterstock;
38tr: Karl Kanal/istockphoto;
40–41tc: Craig Hansen/istockphoto;
40bl: Araldo de Luca/corbis;
42–43bl: Sigurgeir Jonasson, Frank Lane Picture Agency/corbis;
43tl: Iberto Garcia/corbis; **44**b: David Watkins/shutterstock;
44bl: Hans Strand/corbis; **45**br: Douglas Peebles/corbis;
45tl: Dave G. Houser/corbis; **46**br: Phototake Inc/photolibrary;
46tl: Burstein Collection/corbis; **47**t: Pacific Stock/photolibrary;
47bl, **48**bl, **49**br, **50**tr: Science Photo Library/photolibrary;
53tl: Karel de Pauw/alamy